REFUSE TO LOSE

Demetria Buie

Published By:

DBPUBLICATIONS

Printed in the United States of America

DEDICATION
TO MY GRANDMA

The Broken Girl

I dedicate this book to women who was once, like me, were broken, confused, had low self-esteem, a dysfunctional home, felt lonely, settled, unforgiveness, over-eating, overweight, depressed, and tried to please everyone. It took many years for me to reach my moment of true self-love. I never knew about self-love or was taught about it, and if I did hear it, I didn't understand it, or I was stuck in tradition. My hope for you is that you no longer Live in bondage, or a dark and sad place. You no longer ask permission to Live, dream, fly-high, or become so needy & a attention seeker. I hope that after you finish this book of a long journey of suffering, that you keep pushing forward.

That you will wake up one day and be FREE too. You may say I don't need your help or steps because Jesus is all I need. Then yelp! You will stay in that same place. Jesus wasn't all

Jesus needed while he was here on earth; that's why he had disciples. I hope your circumstances change, your circle changes, and your mindset and wellness changes. But most importantly SELF-LOVE. It attracts Love. You no longer have Live in fear. Fear is not Love.

Over the year, I've grown so much. I've evolved. I've learned as I look at myself today. I don't ask God why me. Anymore. I know now I needed to go through that broken girl to BECOME and still become the person I have ever seen yet. So, I dedicate this book to the Broken Girl. But after grabbing and reading my new book, "From Broken Woman To Business Woman," Speak it today that you are no longer broken, at the end of that book; I have some tips and strategies to help you along your journey!!

REMEMBER: I wrote this book at age 25 I'm 37 years old now. So much has happened & Changed. Wisdom has become my portion!!

"He gives strength to the weary and increases the power of the weak. Even youths grow tired and weary, and young men stumble and fall, but those who hope in the LORD will renew their strength. They will soar on wings like eagles; they will run and not grow weary; they will walk and not be faint"
(Isaiah 40: 29-31).

TABLE OF CONTENTS

Demetria Buie is a dedicated, loving mother to her son. Despite being an accomplished entrepreneur, Buie holds her title as 'mother' most dear to her heart. As a youth, she faced her fair share of challenges. Buie dropped out of junior high school, ultimately leaving her small town in Louisiana at eighteen years old, and moved to Richmond, Virginia. Despite dropping out of school, she never gave up. Buie received her

GED at twenty-three and then pursued an acting degree at John Tyler Community College. She then obtained employment after college but was left unfulfilled by her work. As a result, she walked off her job in 2013 and has yet to look back. She has transformed her life and become a well-reputed entrepreneur in her community. Buie is an accomplished author and magazine owner (over 55 published books+ issues), publisher, business owner, Magazine owner, life-story coach, Lupus Supporter, & international speaker. She was recently named 2018 Female Entrepreneur of the Year. Her success stems from her innate mindset of transforming obstacles into opportunities. Buie has worked with Cora Jake's Coleman as her mentor, has been Featured on LupusLA and KNOE News, & was the Keynote Speaker in Toronto, Canada, for the "Turning Dreams Into Reality" Conference.

Buie's road to success was full of difficulties. At one point, she found herself homeless, depressed, and suicidal. At this point, Buie learned to reconstruct her pain into passion. She began writing her first book, an autobiography titled Refuse to Lose, in 2009. Her newly found optimism and relentless pursuit of her new journey reignited her spirit. Buie found purpose, motivation, and hope for a better future. Realizing that her past did not have to define her future, she knew she was destined for bigger and better things. Buie decided to dedicate her time to helping others and empowering those who have been dealt a rough hand, especially women. Empowering others is how Buie makes a difference in the lives of others. She recently hosted her first "over 40 Conferences, Pop-Ups, & Retreats " to inspire women. Her speaking abilities and authentic experiences captivate her audience. Buie now works tirelessly to help others achieve the same mindset. Stay Whole & Well.

"We cannot change the events that have occurred in our past — in some instances, we may not have had much choice in them, but we do have the power to create our future," I Refuse to Lose–Demetria Buie.

INTRODUCTION

SOME QUESTIONS TO PONDER ...

Were you there when it hit you? It hit you hard, didn't it? Did it hurt? Did you feel it? Do you remember it? How often do you think about it? Like being born... did you ever think that was a mistake? Oh, and the past... can't you stop thinking about it? Did you ever ask yourself WHY? Why did this have to happen to me? Why would an older, more mature adult take, or try to take, a child's innocence? Why do a mother and father fail to protect their children from danger?

Has there ever been a time in your life when you felt as if you should not be in this world? Have you ever felt you were over something, but you were not because the pain kept coming back? Have you ever been rejected over and over again? Have you turned loneliness into looking for a mate to fulfill the voids in your life from what you did not get from your parents? Have you ever made so many mistakes that you cannot forgive yourself? Have you ever felt like a helpless little boy or girl walking down a lonely path?

Well, I have. I have been there. Yes, it hit me hard, it hurt, I felt it, I remember it, and I think about it.

This is my story...

1

Chapter One

AS A CHILD

As a child growing up in the small town of Rayville, Louisiana, I did not appear to have any worries. I stayed to myself and never really talked to anyone. I loved my mom and dad. I looked up to my sisters and other friends of the family. Some of my family members were so mean to me, and I did not understand why, but I did know that it hurt me deeply. I held a lot inside of me then, but not anymore…

My father was weird. I never talked to him much, not until I became a teenager. He and my mom fought and argued all the time. When they separated, I blamed myself so much for it. Why? Because it seemed that everything was starting to go smoothly—no fighting or arguing—and then, one day, I was talking to a guy on the phone… The house was so quiet, and I did not want my parents to hear me talking to the guy, so I tried to cover it up by asking my dad questions. I began to bring up old stuff like, "Dad, why did you come in so late last night?" Then my mom got upset at my dad, and they started to argue again. My motive was to have a private conversation on the phone and keep my parents from hearing it, but that day things went in another direction and to another level. My parents began to fight and argue. My father hit my mother, called the police, and then ran down the street. When the police finally came, my father was getting ready to shoot my mom and me, but the police stopped him. My father threatened to come back and burn our house when he was being arrested,. I began to scream, and my mom was so scared that she grabbed me as the police took him away. He was gone for good, or so we thought. After that, my mom and dad broke up. They were together for twenty-one years and never married. I always thought they were married, but they weren't.

While in pre-school, I loved some of the things we did there. I really did not understand why I had to go to school. No one ever told me the reason why. I was held back in the first and fourth grades. At that time, I did not even understand why. I am not sure if I even cared. At that time, no one ever told me to do homework in my house. I was only told, "When you get home, sandwich meat (pressed ham) is in the refrigerator, and lock the door. Don't answer the door if anyone knocks." Basically, I would do whatever I wanted. No one ever told me to do homework or asked me to review my assignments. My mom was always gone, playing cards… oh boy.

I used to play, smile, and have fun with other kids. All I did was play outside. I had about three friends who lived across the street, but we really did not get along. Sometimes we would talk about each other and fight, which at my house was nothing new. The house we lived in was not the perfect home. We barely had hot water. As I said, it was not the perfect home, but I made it home. I would sit and have visions of homes, and I would always get magazines and look at the nice furniture, rugs, cabinets, and beautiful homes. I would say to myself, "We are going to have that." I would show and tell my friends these things, but they would only laugh at me. No one knew about my gifts and talents.

I was in many activities when I was a child, like gymnastics and cheerleading, and I was a member of the Stingerettes dancers. At church, I sang in the choir. Often, I was asked to sing a solo part. I was so creative. I started writing at the age of nine. I loved to write, whether the words were spelled correctly or not or if the handwriting was poor. I would write songs and sing them, but I was not a very good singer.

No one would take the time to get to know me and see who I really was. I had no one to talk to, so I would talk to this "man," His name was GOD (LOL ... funny, huh? That's what I said. He turned out to be so much more than just a man. I would just believe God for stuff even when I could not see it. I would still be excited as He had already given it to me. WOW! What a feeling! That belief did not stop.

I always stayed in trouble when I was younger... all the time. I never really had my sisters around. I was about 8 or 9 years old, and they had already moved out of the house. In my house, there was a lot of -calling and nasty things being said and watched. I got spankings a lot and stayed in trouble. I had to get it from someone, right? As a youth, I never really smiled at all. I had nothing to smile about. I did not feel any love at all, especially not from my mother. She fed, clothed, and gave me a roof over my head. But that is what she was supposed to do, right? I had no real relationship with her. I felt like she was not my mother but just a stranger I lived with. I could never really talk to her like a mother and daughter are supposed to do.

I can remember in the second grade when I had a test at school. I studied for over a week. I had never made good grades before this particular time. I said, "I can do this." We finally had the test at school that morning. I got my test scores before school was out, and I scored an A+ 100!!! I was on the bus and just could not wait to get home. I could not sit still on the bus seat. I got off the bus and ran home. I could not wait to show my mom that paper. I was so excited. When I got home to show her the paper, I said, "Look, look!" but she never looked at the paper. She just ignored me and kept talking to her friends who were there. She was playing cards and gambling. There were always a lot of people in our house. When I finally saw that she would not pay attention, I walked away sad after tapping on her leg so many times. I threw the paper in the trash, went outside, and played in the mud with a stick. I did not care anymore about anything, especially school.

My dad always told me, "I want you to remember one thing if you do not remember anything else: I will always love you." We never had a relationship. He never showed love. He would read the Bible all the time but never lived it. My dad was always getting arrested. When I was younger, I saw him at the prison, but I could not hug him because I did not have proper identification. I saw him through a window. He was chained from his hands to his feet. He could barely walk. He saw me and waved, and I waved back. I was so happy to see him.

I was twelve years old when I had my first boyfriend. I met him at the skating rink. He was that young thug type of guy. He was two years older than me, but he always treated me well.

He really liked me. I knew he did because he once rode his bike a long way from his house to mine. To get to my house from his in a car takes about 30 to 40 minutes. When he showed up at my house, I was so shocked. Looking back, I was too young to have a boyfriend but did not have anyone to tell me I was not doing the right thing. My mom liked him. Even his mom came and picked me up a couple of times to go to the movies and their family reunion. He was always talking back to his mom. I guess I was used to all kinds of things like that happening. I tried to encourage him not to treat his mother that way. He had a mother who was trying to be there for him and tell him the right thing to do. She would take him to school and love him unconditionally. At that time, I wished I had that. He just did not know how it felt not to have that.

At the age of 14, I moved to Virginia. My boyfriend did not want me to move, but I did. I wanted to escape my mother, so I stayed with my sisters and went to school there. I talked to him every day until I met other, more advanced girls. I fell off with my boyfriend and started doing my own thing. There were cuter guys in Virginia; my boyfriend and I lived too far away from each other. He cried and was upset with me, but I had to move on because other things started to excite me.

Living with my sisters was not so good. There were still no role models around me. I felt like I was just there to be there. I started getting in trouble at school. I found a new friend who knew the ropes. I was 14 and talking to guys who were 20 and 23 years old. The guys did not know how old my friend and I were because we lied about our ages. My sisters accused me of many things I was not doing. I guess they did many things in their lifetime and thought I was like them. WRONG. Shortly after living in Virginia for only one year, my sisters sent me back home and said that I could not come back until I turned 18 years old. I did not want to go initially, but I did not have much choice.

Once I got on the bus going home, I was glad but confused. Inside me, I did not know which way I was going. I was so young, and I was faced with some hard decisions. Things were happening that I had no control over, and I did not know how to fix them. I am telling all parents to leave that comfortable door open for their children to talk to you about anything... sex, boys, school, or personal feelings. Never make them feel like outsiders because if you do, they will get what they are looking for outside of the house.

After returning home, I never talked to or heard from my dad until months later. I did not think he even cared about me.

I still did not do well in school. One morning, my sister came in and told my mom I was not doing well and would not make it. She said it in such a sad way as if someone had died. From that point on, I began to think I would not make it. I felt like I was nothing. I was 16 years old and going through life not understanding why no one ever believed in me. No one ever told me I was somebody and would make it. Why didn't I have a family that hugged me and told me I was pretty? Why didn't I get what I needed in life? Why didn't anyone ever tell me that God really loved me?

One day I met a new friend, and I told him the things that were going on in my life, and he said, "Yeah, okay. Dee, do you remember what God said about that?"

I said, "No." I had gotten so caught up in my own problems, other people's problems, and the things around me that I had forgotten all about God, what He was saying to me, and what His word said in the Bible. "Though my father and mother forsake me, the LORD will take care of me" (Psalm 27:10). Wow! When my friend told me that, I said, "Wow, I forgot about that." He told me to look up the scripture for myself and re-read it. It all applied to my life.

I remember when I was in Walmart one day. I only had one thing to purchase and was first in line. A woman came down the line and got right in front of me and did not say anything. She was in front of me, and her husband was behind me, and he was calling her names, but she kept telling him, "Come on up here!"

I just said to myself, "Look at this!" I wanted to get out of the line and go to the other cashier, but I was tired of people feeling like they could do me any way, so I stayed there. I put my one thing on the counter, and she looked at me and said, "I was here first!"

She had one of those things that you talk with when you can't talk. She was saying all kinds of nasty stuff to me. I wanted to take that machine and shove it down her throat, but I just said, "Whatever!" and walked off. As they were going out of the store, they were laughing. They thought the situation was funny, but I didn't. I had to remember who I was and that

I had wrong thinking. That night, I had to repent and pray for her and myself. Whenever I thought about that situation, I told myself that God has been taking care of me my whole life.

~~~~~~~~~~~~

Remember that God is there when people seem to forsake you, even your family, and they are not there to listen to you. He said, "I'll be the one who takes care of you." He was the one who has taken care of me all along, and He will still be the one who cares for me.

Life really does get hard. Not having someone in your life can also be hard, especially for those who want to be married, especially when it seems like that right guy or girl hasn't come along. It is also hard when you have children and can barely pay your bills. It takes money to live… but God, God promises to take care of you and supply all of your needs. You have to believe that. Even though we may have to go through some things and have tests, remember that ONLY THE STRONG WILL SURVIVE. So what if your mom, dad, husband, brother, neighbor, aunt, uncle, cousin, boyfriend, best friend, step-parent, or coworker has done you wrong? It is time to move on, even if you have to cry. I got to the point where I was all cried out. You have to look in the mirror and see that you are beautiful. No one can take it that way. Remember, you have power over your life. You have the power to make a difference in your life.

I once read a book entitled *Healed without Scars*. It is an awesome book by David Evans. In it, he said, THE PAST HAS NO POWER OVER YOUR FUTURE. What a powerful word! The past... your past, has no power over your future. Take that and run with it. Don't let anyone tell you differently. What has happened in your past has nothing to do with where you are going. Wash it away, and throw it in the trash. The past is old news. Move on; you have to. You cannot stay in the past. You are strong. Don't lose what you believe in... trials may come your way, but with the Lord, YOU will be in peace. You can't change what has happened in the past, but you can change your future.

WHAT COMES OUT OF YOUR MOUTH

Do you take the things you say seriously? Do you think before you speak? Really? Well, if you do not, you should. The tongue is a very powerful tool. TOOL? Yes, tool; and you have to know how to use it.

I can recall when I did not have a place to live, and lived from place to place. Not having your own space is a terrible thing. It is not a good feeling. Things did not look so great for me. Every morning, when I awoke, I would say that I would have my own place again, and in the evenings, I would worship. When I worshipped, I began to speak those things that were not as though they were.

At times, it may look like what you are speaking is not going to happen. But, it will in due time. The Bible says that life and death are in the power of the tongue. Be careful what you say to yourself and what you say to others. People know you by the words that come out of your mouth. I spoke so much and confessed loudly that I was going to have my own place again.

Even though I did not see it right away, I believed it. About five months later, I was in my own place. That night, I walked around my apartment (after three years of not having my own place to live). It was amazing to have my own place again; I could not believe it. I really took what I said more seriously than ever before. For example, when I was 18 years old, getting ready to leave my mom, I said I wanted a change in my life... and I got it. Make sure that you think before you speak. Your words mean a lot. Make sure you speak life and think positively. It will make a difference in your life.

FINDING THE REAL YOU

We all endure pain. Even rich people who seem to have it all, go to the best schools, wear designer clothes, and drive the best cars, still endure pain. When their parents have to work so that they and their children have nothing but the best of the best, they still endure pain. I met a lot of students at school who seemed to be one way, but they really were another way. They acted as if they were better just because their parents had money. But, all along, they were unhappy. So, they had to treat others a certain way to make themselves feel good about who they were. You should treat people as you want to be treated. But wait for a second... some people do not even know how they should be treated, so they do not know how to treat others. Many people do not value themselves. Instead, they cover up and pretend to be someone they are not.

It is okay to be you. Get pride out of the way because it can hold you back from being yourself. I know that many rich

13

people cover up their problems, or others see the rich as having money and think they do not have any problems. Many rich people tend to act like everything is okay in their lives, but deep down inside them, it is not. People cover up by wearing high-priced clothes, make-up, and much more. You can only cover up for so long. You cannot hide behind the darkness forever because, eventually, it will all come into the light.

Whether you are wealthy or not, you do not have to pretend to be someone else just to make yourself feel good. Being honest about who you are and where you come from is okay. We all experience pain in our lives. There is nothing to be ashamed of or to cover up. More people can be healed by revealing their true selves.

~~~~~~~~~~~~

Chapter Two

INTRUSION

rowing up was not always easy for me. I had thoughts of suicide and wished my mother was dead because, in that house, she was never a mother to me. She cursed me out a lot and called me names. She would always call me ugly. She would say she was joking, but in my mind, I believed it. I just hated her so much. She was no kind of role model for me. One thing I knew was that I did not want to be anything like her. The love, affection, and care I did not get from my parents caused me to turn into men's arms. I had to get my love from somewhere, right? Well, little did I know I was headed down the wrong path. What I did know was that I wanted to be loved.

My dad's not around hurt me so much. By this time, he began to sell drugs heavily. He was a big-time dealer. He brought me radios and hundreds of dollars all of the time. Boy, I was so happy. I would spend the money one day at Walmart and restaurants. I loved my dad so much; I believe he loved me too. He just did not know how to show it or do what he was supposed to do. I believe my mother also loved me but did not know how to be a mother. I knew it had to be God watching over me and guiding me through my life. He allowed me to go through this for a reason.

We have a pretty large family. They were people I initially trusted, but they were always talking about each other, never got along, and were so dysfunctional. It came to a point where I never trusted a living soul again… and my family, definitely not.

One morning, I was lying on the couch, and someone knocked at the door. My mother was in her room sleeping. I did not want to get the door because I was tired. They kept on knocking, so I finally got to the door. It was my uncle, my aunt's husband. He wanted my mom so he could either give something to her or get something from her. When he came back up the hall from my mother's bedroom and headed for the door, he stopped because he wanted more. He patted me on the head as I was lying on the couch and said goodbye. Then, he patted me again and said goodbye again. I saw him look down the hallway toward my mom's bedroom, and then he took his patting a bit further. He went down into my shirt, touched my breasts, and tried to do even more. As he tried to put his hand over my mouth, I started screaming, "Mom! Mom! Mom!"

Then, he started to put his finger to his mouth and said, "Shhhh!" He was trying to tell me to be quiet. My mom finally came running in as I continued to scream about what he was doing to me. He started waving his hands from side to side and said, "No! No!" My mom told him to get out. He left, and I was so scared I went into the kitchen and got a knife. My mom called my aunt and told her what had happened but, my aunt did not believe what my mother was saying. My aunt and her daughter said I was lying. Later on, I found out that he had raped multiple women in the past. Some of the women were our family members. Still today, my aunt is with him. I believe she is just in denial and afraid of being alone. My mom still cooks for my aunt and everything. Man, if someone did that to my daughter, I would have a hard time cooking for them or doing anything for them… but that is just how my mom is with people.

I felt no love from anyone. I began to talk to multiple men, mostly older men, but some were young. They would tell me things that I longed for my mother and father to say to me. When they would say, "Oh wow, you are so cute and beautiful," that is what hit the spot. My eyes enhanced, and my heart opened. That is what I needed to hear, and that is what I wanted. I had no worries for a while because I was getting what I needed from the guys at school. What I liked was much attention. They would say, "Oh, you are so fine." One guy would tell me he was going to marry me. To me, I needed more love and closeness. I did not want to feel or be alone again.

I soon got involved in other activities with these guys, like intimacy. In my mind, I knew that was all they wanted, but when I was in a moment of pleasure, it felt like closeness. It felt like I could hear, "you are not alone," "I am here for you," and "I love you." I needed to feel that over and over and over again. So, if that is what I needed, I had to do it over and over and over again. Even if it was only for a minute, it was a minute of not being alone. I loved not feeling alone.

About four years later, I was finally dating this guy I had been waiting a year for, but little did I know that it was not what I thought it would be. Have you ever been in a place where you did not want to be alone? Do you feel that way now? Most of the time, we settle for less and know that we deserve better. But, it is that loneliness that just will not let you. Well, this love of my life and I started dating. I was in relationship after relationship.

Have you ever found yourself in one relationship after another? You have no time for yourself or to get to know yourself. You have babies after babies because you just have to be with someone. You just have to be with someone because you are used to being with someone. But, think for a moment… Do you think it is time for you to spend some time with yourself and get to know and love yourself??? The reason why you are in relationship after relationship is that you do not even know yourself. You do not even know what you want. What are your goals in life? Are you working on them? What about school and caring for your kids first? Are you trying to get pregnant on purpose just to keep him or because you think it will change him? Or, have you even lied to him about being pregnant? Not cool!!! When are you going to take the time out for yourself? Are you just afraid of being alone? Who else will love being around you if you do not love being around yourself? Believe me; it becomes easier and easier each day when you begin to love yourself.

Chapter Three

MY LIFE TOOK
A FAST TURN ON ME

All the stuff I was in and living the way I was living was taking me down the wrong path. I had been in GED school for about three years. I was not doing anything with my life. I was smoking and drinking at school with other students. I was not getting along with my mom. I would get in fights at school all of the time. I had a "beef" with just about everybody. I was associating with different people who were not good for me. I had low self-esteem, and I did not love myself. I never knew how to dress up and look cute and never spoke to anyone. I always walked around with my head low; all I ever wore were plaid shirts. I had no life at all.

In my house, guys would come and go. I had guys spending the night, and my mom knew it. She was in denial. And, at GED school, we did nothing but watch porn with our teachers. We did not do any homework. At the end of the school year, many of us found out that the lady who was our teacher was sleeping with other female students. More teachers were doing it also. Man, it was a disaster. We did anything and everything under the sun. A lot of students would go around the school and smoke marijuana. I was on my way to destruction and headed straight to the pit of hell… but God's hands were on me, even when I did not know it. Being with the most popular guy every other girl wanted to be with was a great feeling. He did choose me for a little while. With all this mess I was already in, it did not appear that things were getting any better for me. Then, my dad really began to get sick. My dad came around, but he could not walk. He said he could, but never got out of the "Hover Round." After the separation, my mom and dad got along better. He changed a lot. He started going to church in the Hover Round. I did not really talk to him much, and my boyfriend was in Iraq.

When my boyfriend finally came home, I got a call from my dad's sister at the same time to tell me that my dad was in the hospital and that, this time, it did not look so good. My dad had a girlfriend, but he treated her so wrong. Let me tell you, once, she was in the bathroom about to douche, and he told her that someone wanted her outside, but no one wanted her. He got one of his buddies to act like he was selling something. While his girlfriend was outside, my dad took the douche bottle, poured out the water, put rubbing alcohol in it, and ran out of the bathroom. When she returned to use the product, she started screaming, and they had to rush her to the hospital. My dad laughed about it so much. I did not think it was funny at all. He had a dog and named the dog after his girlfriend. He would whistle to the dog and call the dog her name, and then he would laugh about it. But when he started going to church, I knew nothing about it.

When we saw him in the hospital, he was on life support. The doctors said he had been trying to pull the plug. When my fourth sister went to see him, he asked her to pull the plug. She may saw more than me. When I saw him, he was asleep and barely hanging on. His sister tried to wake him up for me, but he did not wake up. That Christmas morning, we went up to see him and walked into the room. We thought he was doing better, but he wasn't. He died that Christmas morning at 10 a.m., and we did not even know. The doctor said fast, "Oh yeah, he died around 10 this morning." Then the doctor threw the covers back over my dad's face like he was nothing. I never did touch my dad. My mom, my sister, and her friends who were present did touch him. We left, and it was a sad day for me.

Things did not get any better when I got home. I told my adorable boyfriend that my dad had just died. He sat on the bed with no words to say, then left. Not only did he leave me, he left me for another woman. He dropped out of school, and the lady he left me for was much older. She had children and her own home; he did not have any children. I did not have any friends who came to visit me. But this was the man I said would never leave, never hurt me, and that he would marry and love me until the end.

Chapter Four

SEEKING TO BE LOVED

My life was not getting any better. I wanted out, and I had to find a way. In my mind, I had two choices … suicide or leaving my mother. I planned suicide. I had a lot of pills, and I lined them up to take them. Even though I had lots of problems taking pills, that day in my room, it was not going to be a problem. I was ready to go. I asked my sister, two days earlier, to allow me to come back to live with her, go to school, and do something with my life. I did not get a response from her until the day I planned the suicide. When I had all the pills lined up and ready to go, I wrote a note saying, "My mom never loved me, God never showed me He cared, and I never had any sisters to look up to. I never felt loved, so why stay here? No more pain for me." I kept hearing my mom call me, but I ignored her. I was trying to take myself out.

She then came to the door and said, "Your sister said that you can come to stay with her, and the bus ticket will be there in the morning." In my head, that was good, but I still did not know if I could continue living. So, she started knocking on the door, and I opened it. She was smiling, but I knew she did not want me to leave. I did not even think she saw the redness under my eyes from the tears and the pain I was having. I went into the bathroom and lay in the tub. She left and said she was going to play cards, that there was sandwich meat (pressed ham) in the refrigerator, and that I was not to let anyone in the house because she had her key. I lay in the bathtub for hours. The next morning I left, taking my little clothes and leaving everything else behind. My mom and her friend dropped me off at the bus station. I left without saying goodbye to anyone. I never looked back and have only been back once since then.

Twenty-four hours on that bus was a long time to get to Virginia, where I was supposed to be. This was my chance, my change. Never in my life did I think I would go through what I went through moving to Virginia. I got there but did I go back to school? No. Once again, still wanting to feel loved, I did not get what I needed. I had a mind of my own but did not know how to use it. I was always doing what other people wanted me to and trying to please them. There I was, once again, on a date with some guy I met on the chat line.

I thought it would be different. I thought the guys in Virginia told the truth and treated you better, but, I guess my focus was still on trying to be loved because I had never felt it before. I looked to men to get my love because they showed it. Even if it was a lie or fake, they showed it. It is not just men who hurt women in relationships; women do it, also.

Going to Virginia was a big change for me. I was now 18 years old and did not know how to drive. My dad promised to teach me, but I could not rely on that anymore, could I? I had no education and no experience with living on my own. I listened to my sisters as they told me what to do, when, and how to do it, especially my third sister... and I did it. She is a very controlling person anyway. I found myself a job and even began to drive. My third sister did help me to do that. I did not want to, but you had to have transportation living there. This was a difficult task for me. No one offered the opportunity to teach me what I needed to know about life and living once I was an adult; everyone assumed I already knew.

As things progressed, my life did not take the high way I had planned in my head. Living with my sisters in Virginia was no different from living with my mom at home. My third sister was almost the worst. She screamed all the time for no reason and only screamed at me. She only screamed at my sisters a couple of times. I think I cried more than the Mississippi River runs. I think I was hurt even more by living with my sister. I was downgraded and talked about because I did not have my high school diploma or GED. My sisters told me I was not doing anything with my life. One time, we went out to have dinner, and my mom was there. My third sister told me that I was a nobody because I was going out to speak and help at a group home. She told me I could not do that because I did not have my GED. My mom never defended me, never. She never said anything but would love to call me and tell me to treat my sisters right, even though she knew I was not doing anything to them. Everything always fell back on me. She never would listen to my side of the story. Because my sister allowed me to live with her when I moved there, she used that to her advantage. Hurting someone's feelings and making them cry over and over again when you know that you are hurting them now is abuse. When I got tired of the abuse, I started speaking for myself, and I would call my mom on the phone and try to tell her what was going on, but she would only say, "Oh, how are you gonna sit up there and say that after all, she is doing for you? Your sister is giving you money and letting you stay at her house. You should be ashamed of yourself. I don't want to hear it!!! BYE!" and then she would hang up the phone.

Oftentimes, you have to be careful whom you let do for you, even your family because they will hang it over your head. When a person does something for you from their heart, they do not keep bringing it up in your face all the time, trying to make you feel guilty. Never allow anyone to have that much control over you. It could leave you in bondage for a very long time.

Living with my sister was bad enough for me. I had to make a move again. When it is time to make a move, a lot of people question it. Me, I think about it and do it. I was starting to know that I did not want people treating me any kind of way anymore. That was the reason why I left my mother's home. I wanted to escape all the cursing, screaming, negativity, and fear. I wanted peace but could not seem to find it. So, I moved out of my third sister's home, and my fourth sister and I moved in together. That was not so pleasant either, but it was a little better. I was always the one who was picked on at the dinner table. When my other sisters would visit, they would always ask me, "What are you going to do with yourself? You are not going anywhere in your life."

They would look at each other and say, "I don't know what she is going to do with herself." They would ask me all of the time, "When are you going to go back to school and get your GED?" and "When you go back to school, we are going to give you one thousand dollars … we will be so happy." My mother promised me a laptop and so much more if I got my GED. Did that happen?

My sisters and other family members were not supportive. They degraded me with every word, slightly destroying my limited self-esteem. My horrifying and damaging encounters increased, among other things. I was getting drunk every weekend on any kind of alcohol I could get my hands on. See, I met a lot of guys who loved women who loved to drink, have fun, and let loose. Those types of guys were so easy to find. They would make you feel so loved and wanted.

I wanted a change but did not know what kind. I knew I did not want to do the things I was doing anymore. I was getting tired of the same ole guys doing the same things repeatedly that I had been doing my entire life. I was getting nowhere, I thought to myself. So I thought that maybe if I had a child, that would solve all of my problems, and I would be loved by my child and not be alone. I thought that whatever man I had my child by would also change and want to be with me for the rest of my life and finally love me for me, giving me the love that I always wanted and had been looking for... but that never happened. I tried and tried, and even at times, I lied to some guy about being pregnant. That was so wrong. I believe I really hurt him, but he had to remember that he hurt me first, then played with my feelings and used me. He did not want anything to do with me, so I had to find a way to hurt and pay him back. When I told him I was pregnant, that was my payback because there were nights that he did not sleep because he was sweating through the night with worry. He did not know how to go through the day and could hardly work, leaving early and giving me good attention by treating me like I was his world. He started calling me every morning. I told myself that this is what it takes to get him to treat me right… but that was not true.

I came to realize that you cannot change people. If they change for you, it is only temporary. Never try to change a person. For the men, I say never let hips, thighs, butts, and breasts make you. Get to know that woman's heart and not just her body. If you continue that way, you will end up in a lot of trouble with a woman you wish you had no part of. Try getting to know her and who she really is from the inside out.

I realized that many men like drama girls and to be treated wrong because that is all that they are used to. They do not know what it is like to be treated like a king. We all have to present ourselves how we want people to view us. We have all made mistakes and do not always have them together.

How do you make that move away from being in abusive relationships, having low self-esteem, bitterness, loneliness, unforgiveness, jealousy, strife, uncertainties about life, confusion, always dealing with rejection, gossip, the judgment of others, lies, excuses, worrying, anger, fear, stress to the point of weight and hair loss, complaining, ungratefulness, inability to deal with failure, relationship problems, bad attitudes, can't take correction, doubt, and being a controlling person?

Read on …

Chapter Five

FINDING
THE GOOD IN THE EVIL

At times, it looks like we are having fun in our lives. I thought I knew what I wanted and where I was headed. But do you know that your life can change in the heat of the moment, anytime, and anywhere? All the time, I never thought my life would or could change overnight. It is funny how God has His ways of getting our attention and shifting things around in our lives.

I can remember how I used to drink all of the time. Nothing bad ever happened when I did. I would drink to get a lot of things off of my mind. That is what I thought the drinking was doing. I would drink really fast to get drunk quickly because when I was drunk, I felt no pain. It was a feeling that made me forget everything. That "buzz" made me lie down or fall out. That is what I always liked to feel. I was dealing with so much in my life and never knew when the pain would end.

At that time, I was trying to get to know God, but it felt like I just could not get to Him, or He was not listening when I said, "Lord, I want to be saved, and I want to live right. Please fix what is going on with my family and me." I guess I wanted an answer right then and there or to see something happen. I did not want to stop drinking because drinking made the pain end, but only for that moment. I called it TEMPORARY LOVE, and that is exactly what it was, but I was tired of temporary things in my life.

When my fourth sister and I were roommates, this light-skinned, pretty guy lived upstairs from us. Everybody wanted to have him. I guess so. He was one of those "pretty boys." I would often see him and speak, but one morning we both were walking out at the same time on our way to work, and we just started talking. You know, that talk like, "How long have you been living here?" "Where are you from?" "Do you like it here?"

He replied, "There is not too much to do." Since I was not from Richmond, Virginia, he knew more than me. He suggested, "Let me show you around, and maybe we can hang out sometimes."

I said, "Sure, why not?" We both agreed to meet when we got off work around the same time. Later that evening, he came over to my apartment. We talked and drank. He brought liquor over, and he also had marijuana with him. I was not down with the marijuana, but I did not care about him smoking it in my apartment. We were both getting drunk. I cannot remember when we even started drinking (after that night, things were never the same for me). We also smoked Black and Milds all night. I noticed that he started kissing me. The next thing I knew, I was passed out because I was so drunk. A couple of hours later, I woke up and could barely open my eyes. I did not know what was going on. I started crying, and then I started screaming. He did not know what to do. He was holding my arm while I was all over the floor. I could remember him being so afraid and asking if I was okay. I did not know what was going on. I was drunk, but something else was happening. I started shaking, and he dragged me, trying to put me back into the bed. He finally did, but I was still crying. I was sweating as I had just run a 10K. As he wiped my forehead, I could feel his hands shaking. From what I knew, he was a gentleman... ha!!! I knew nothing about this guy except his name and that he lived upstairs. He talked to me until I fell asleep.

I woke up early the next morning with a terrible hangover. I had gotten drunk many times but had never felt that way before. I woke up and could barely get out of bed. Looking down, I saw five bottles of vodka on the floor and three cans of beer. They were all empty. I started throwing up non-stop. I did not know what had happened to me the night before at all. I needed to locate this guy to ask him what had happened. So, with a towel over my head, I walked upstairs. I was sick and confused and did not even go to work. I knocked on his door, and he came with a towel over his neck, saying, "Man, I do not know what happened to you, but I was scared."

I said, "I know."

He said, "Girl, you do not even seem like a real drinker or smoker. I know women that really get down like that, and it ain't you." I paused and thought about it. He was walking back and forth with a towel over his neck. I asked him what had happened. He took the towel off and showed me all the "hickies" on his neck. He was a light-skinned guy, so the marks really showed up.

I was like, "Wow!" I asked him why he seemed so nervous.

He said, "My girlfriend is on her way over, and I have hickies all over my neck."

My mouth dropped, and I said, "Wow! You did not tell me you had a girlfriend."

He said, "Yeah, yeah. Well, we ain't doing so good."

I left immediately, and throughout that day, something changed in me. I kept thinking that I did not want another drink in my life again. I did not have a taste for it anymore. I had never gotten that sick before and fallen out. For some reason, I prayed for that moment because I was also missing my dad. I wanted to talk to him. I was only 19 years old and so confused. I was thinking about my life and feeling like I was such a huge mess-up. I did not know how to fix anything. Everything that happened to me, I felt, was entirely my fault. That day I threw away all the liquor and beer I had in my house. I felt as though I had a different mindset. I knew that I did not want to drink my problems away anymore. The next day at work, I gave all of those Black and Milds away. I felt good about it. On my lunch break, I started reading my Bible. I did not know too much about what I was reading. I just thought I would start somewhere. I started reading what was in red. It was the things Jesus said. I tried to understand it. I believe all that happened so that God could get my attention. I knew that God had delivered me from those bad habits because I prayed and asked Him to, and He did it in His own time. I know that it was God because I am now 25 years old and have not taken a drink since that night. I have no desire to drink at all. I even hate being around and smelling liquor.

Anything that you ask God for, with a pure heart, and you believe it in your heart; it does not matter what kind of state you are in; if you ask Him and wait on Him, He will deliver you from your habits. But first, you must want it and be ready when the time comes.

One day, I simply woke up and experienced a life-altering revelation. I literally thanked my family and friends for their devastating treatment and comments. My life was a stormy disaster. I longed for change. Every negative event around me made me so emotional and exhausted. "How long do I continue this journey of devastation?" I asked. I was destroying my life with all of the things that I was doing wrong.

"This is not it!" I exclaimed. I must prove them wrong. It was time to pursue my destiny. I stopped drinking, dismissed the craving for masculine affection, and finally realized I was not what I did.

Chapter Six

I AM NOT WHAT I DID

I am not what I did. I recovered through the words of Bishop T.D. Jakes shared in a message I heard on one of his tapes: "Alone But Not Lonely." He said that oftentimes when we feel alone that we are never alone because God is always there for us. When I heard it, I thought to myself, "Is it true that there is a man named Jesus Christ who loves me for me and will never leave nor forsake me and will be there for me until the end?" I started to really think.

I went to church while I was growing up, but no one told me about God and who He really was. While I was walking around looking for love in a man, trying to please other people, and telling them all my business for no reason, love was there for me the entire time. The Lord loves me just the way I am. I knew I no longer had to pretend to be someone I was, not just to feel good about myself.

I wanted to know more about Christ, for real, this time. I started telling my sisters I was a Christian and that I had changed a lot of things in my life. I started praying and asking the Lord to forgive me for everything I have done in my life. I asked Him to help me. I did not know anything about praying; I just did what they said to do on television when I started watching the Word Network. When I told my third sister about this, she said, "How in he## you gonna be a Christian and you don't even go to church, and with the things you have done in your life?" I felt bad when she said that.

The following Sunday, I went to look for a church home. I met a lot of customers from my job at Walmart. I talked to many people at work, and many of them invited me to their church. I went to the church of one of my customers that Sunday. It was okay, but I did not want to become a member. So, I went to another church the next Sunday but did not want to join that one either. I was in a hurry to find a home church. I was invited to another church the next Sunday (you know, everybody wants you at their church). I joined the church. I was happy about joining the spiritual, empowering congregation which became my new family. I was finally accepted and loved (so I thought). I actually participated, once again, in the praise dance ministry. It reminded me of when I used to dance when I was 12 years old when my oldest sister made me go to church. Now I thank her for making me go when I did not want to. I began to smile as I thought about that. God has brought me back to where I belong. I felt good. But, just because I got saved and Christ came into my life, did my life get any easier?

Finally, at 19 years old, I managed to secure my own apartment. But that was sadly short-lived. I did not receive any formal daily life skills training from my parents. I did not know anything about maintaining an apartment or paying bills. I got evicted shortly thereafter. I started to see that church folks talk a lot. In my mind, I thought when you told the people at church that they would not talk about you and would be there for you and love you. I thought these people would not talk behind your back, but I was starting to see them differently. Even the leaders in the church would talk behind your back. Most of the time when I attended church, people were talking about me, and I did not even know it until years later when other church folks would come back and tell me what they said. I was surprised, very much, because I trusted church folks.

I tried to be accepted by others by my appearance, what I did in life, and where I went. I felt like I had to tell my business and every move I made. Even when I messed up, I felt I had to confess my sins and problems to people. I was always looking to be loved by someone. I still did not know that God loved me. The hardest thing was I did not know He was all I needed.

In life, we as people never want to be alone. You have to know your self-worth. I knew I needed to be in tune with and love myself. Many times, when someone is telling you to do things their way and how to live your life, they have complete control over you. I have learned that people love controlling someone else's life… especially in the church. After all that were praying, giving, and faithfulness, I thought that church was where most of my pain would end. Little did I know, this is where the pain really began all over again.

Being hurt and feeling like you cannot be healed is the worst feeling ever. People can tell you all day, "Oh, you don't have to sell your body, and you don't have to settle for this type of man," but in your mind, you say that you do because maybe where you lived and how you were brought up are all that you know. If you have only been around people who curse, then that is all you will know and what you will do. The environment that you are around affects your life. At times, people may say that you do not have to be in that predicament.

However, if you have not seen anything different in your life, then you won't know any different. Then, when you do get exposed to something different, you often do not know how to handle it. A girl I knew did not like anyone doing things for her, like taking her out to eat or anything. People offered to do things for her, and she would always refused. One day, she told me it was because they would "hang it over her head," and she was not used to it.

When all we know is pain, that is what we look for in life—the bad things and the pain.

Take a moment and ask yourself, "DO I WANT A CHANGE, and

HOW DO I MAKE THIS CHANGE IN MY LIFE?"

Chapter Seven

CHURCH HURT

Today, many people are being hurt in the church. It is not fun. I think I got hurt by my church family even more than people in the world. Funny, huh? You have to question whether it is a church or a business because it often seems that money is the priority. I thought there were no liars or backbiters in the church, but if you did wrong, they would talk about you as if they never did any wrong in their own lives. Many things that happen to people in the church are just not fair. I recall how the church people would try to cause confusion. You know, people in the church have the cliques they run with? They only talk to certain people. Often they would go to each other's homes and talk about others in the church. Not only the members but the leaders did it also. LEADERS? YES, leaders. Pastors do it too. Oh! Don't be fooled. It really gets to be sad; it really does. It is a shame that people do not have anything else to do with their time or life!!!

I questioned some things that were happening in the church because I needed to know. So, I talked about it confidentially with a former church member. In no way was I trying to cause confusion. I just wanted to get some questions answered. At that time, I was unable to talk to the pastor. That former member went back and repeated what I said to her family member, who was still a member of the church, and the member went back and told the pastor that I was talking about her. I thought that was so crazy. The pastor never said anything to me about it.

About two weeks later, I got an eviction notice from my apartment complex. I went to the church for help. I talked to the pastor and told her about my situation. She said, "Hmmm, I heard that you were talking about me."

I said, "No, I was not talking about you. I just questioned some things that were going on in the church."

She replied, "Well, that is not what I heard." I began to feel uncomfortable. She then started talking to me with an attitude. I told her that I was being evicted and needed a place to stay or someone to help me keep my current apartment.

She asked me if I had someplace to go, and I said, "My sister, but I am not sure about going back there; she might not let me stay with her."

The pastor said, "Well, I suggest you stay with her and save your money until you can find a place." With the same attitude, she continued writing with her ink pen, never really looking at me at all. I was so hurt I did not know what to say or do. As we walked out of her office, she told me, "The Bible says, don't touch my anointed one and do my prophets no harm." She patted me on the shoulder and walked off. I did not feel that her words were directed at me at all. I felt that I did nothing wrong.

You just have to be careful at all times. You know when something is not right, don't you? Okay, then, just pray about where God wants you to be and not where you want to be. If not, then you will find yourself going through more in life than necessary. JESUS CHRIST never acted like this. For example, how will you shout and say that you love the Lord, and then you can ONLY sit next to certain people in the church? And, all of the gossips, I say stay away from it. Walk away from groups like that. Being with the wrong people gets you nowhere but into trouble, or your name can end up in the middle of something bad you may not have done.

I was always called out in front of the entire church when I did nothing wrong. I could never speak my side of the story. I was always told to be quiet. Most of the church members knew that I did not do anything, but no one ever stood up to speak for me, not even the elders in the church.

You must learn how to pray for yourself. Do not depend on others to do for you all of the time. Know that God hears all of our prayers. The Bible says that the effectual, fervent prayers of the righteous avail much. God is not a respecter of persons. I was always a faithful tither, offering giver, and seed sower. Everything happens for a reason. I could tell you so much more, but I will stop here. Pray about every church you attend and everything you do. Take your time. God will show you where you need to be. Pray for everyone, and God will be pleased with that.

We should always love one another, whether we make a mistake or not. WE ALL HAVE MESSED UP. Learn to forgive (it is hard, I know), as it will make you free. You can sleep better at night and go on with your life.

I knew that God wanted me to go forth and higher. I knew that there were a lot of people who did not want me to go forth. I was in a box for a while. I let everyone and their "momma" control me. They wanted to play momma. I thought about that one day. I left my mom a long time ago. At that time, I was 23 years old, and I had had enough. I was tired of moving from place to place. I was living with my third sister, who ended up putting me out for no reason. I had just lost my job at a daycare, which was her reason. I was sitting on her front punch with my bags, waiting for someone to come and get me. I had a witness who saw it all—her husband. She was the type of person who gave you something, and then, if she got angry with you, she would take it back. I thought she was just like that with me, but she was like that with just about everyone. She was so mean. You could not even talk to her. She was so negative and always screaming about everything.

After sitting on the porch for over an hour, someone from the church finally came and got me. I did not know where I was going to go. I had nowhere to sleep that night. I asked my second sister if I could come back and live with her. She was a little okay with it, but she was in an abusive relationship, so her husband did not want her family there. But hey, when you do not want to be alone, you will do anything for a man. I moved in with her anyway, but eventually, I found a place to live. It was called A House for Women. It was a group home. My second sister and my nephew helped me move there.

I was living under amazingly strict rules. The landlord was a female who was very mean and controlling. Although we were adults, we had to account for our every move. We could only wash clothes on designated days and take showers in the morning. She checked our bedrooms every two days for drugs, condoms, you name it. Yes, that "warlord" examined every move I made. I was suffocating. I had no privacy. It was time to get out, but where was I to go? I had to choose between a house of misery with my sister and a house of dictatorship in that group home. Despite this, while I was at the group home, I did learn a lot.

The landlord showed me how to get my GED. She even took me to a college campus to learn more about college, which was great because I knew nothing... it was all new to me, but it was exciting. I was ready.

Chapter Eight

LOVE FROM A DISTANCE

I got my GED at the age of 23. I chose a major and wanted to go to school for criminal justice. I wanted to be a lawyer.

I ended up leaving the group home and moving in with my fourth sister. Things did not work out there either. This time, after leaving work, I drove to find a safe place to park so I could sleep in my car for a couple of days. I called my mom, but you know her by now, and she was busy playing cards or did not have time to listen to me. To her, I was ALWAYS the wrong one. I found a spot to park and sleep but was too afraid to be there. About 20 minutes later, my cell phone rang. It was one of the ladies from the church. I told her what was going on with me, and she offered to have me come live with her. Boy, was I happy to be in a warm house and take a shower that night? Little did I know that this lady had some serious issues... she was bipolar. I was there for five days, and then I left.

One day, this guy I know called her house for me. I was not there, but the lady answered the phone and asked him if he wanted to leave me a message. He gave her his name and asked her to tell me he had called. His name was the same name as her ex-husband. They had been separated for 12 years. This lady was in her fifties. Her ex-husband was in his sixties. So, when I arrived home at her house, she asked me if I was sleeping with her ex-husband. I thought she was crazy. I did not say anything else to her. She screamed and hollered all that night. I just sat in the room and did not say anything. My friend, who called me, was only 21 years old. I told him about

49

the situation. At least she did apologize, but I left her home the next day.

I moved to a house one cold winter. I was done with my family and my mother. I had a decent job and a car but no place of my own yet. I went to a house and stayed there. It was wintertime, and the house had no heat. It was a shack house. Two other people were living there. How could they live there? Well, I guess they had no other choice, like me. I kept praying and saying, "Lord, I done had enough. Why? Why?" I cried and cried. "Why do I have to go through this?" Those suicidal thoughts reentered my mind. I was so confused.

I met a male friend who wanted to see me. He was very encouraging. In that house, I would not even want a roach to come to see me, but I made it work. I went and bought a heater and lots of blankets from Walmart. I had a TV and a DVD player, the only things I really kept with me through my travels. My first sister sent me $100. I prayed a lot more while I was in that house. It was kind of creepy in that house.

I joined a gym where I could take showers and clean up. About 4 months passed, and I finally heard from my family again. I did not think they wanted to help. They just wanted to be nosey and to see where I was living and what I was doing. My mom wanted to see the house where I was living. I took her to see the house, and after we left, I moved back into my second sister's house. My mom sat in the chair for about ten minutes and started crying, which I thought was funny because she is always crying. She never took the time to listen to me and what really happened. I had no choice. I did what I had to do and went through what I had to go through.

I was so happy when I got baptized at the church, which was my most IMPORTANT day. I kept asking for all of my family to come, but no one showed up. My third sister came, stayed for 5 minutes, then left. A dear older lady-friend came. I really appreciated her coming. After the baptism, she told me that I looked like an angel when I came up out of the water. I smiled, and she frowned. Her eyes had gotten big. She started smiling and laughing. She said, "I have never seen you smile before."

I said, "Oh, okay."

I became exhausted from moving, as I had moved many times over the last three years. My sisters continued to be unkind. They provoked and antagonized me constantly. They denounced my love for God. My mother would visit, yet she did not offer any comfort or protection. I tried so hard to please her. For instance, I never drank or cursed in her presence. It seemed as if I did not have a man beating up on me, had bad relationships, or was drinking or cursing; I could not get a chance for her to listen to me for once in her life.

Another incident happened when my third sister came over and talked about the money I owed her for a car that was never hers. She was already angry that day. She did not just become angry. She said that I think I am better than everyone else. That woman had been mad for a long time, especially when I started attending church. I told her that she would not control me anymore. I would handle my own money and be whom I wanted to be in life. I refused to let her treat me in any kind of way anymore. I finally put my foot down, and she knew she could no longer control me. What hurt her the most was that I was standing up for myself.

She came over and started a fight. She got in my face, grabbed my shirt, and pushed me against the wall. I called the police on her, and then I called my mom and told her not to ever talk to me a day in her life, and I meant it. I said that because I knew that she would not believe me if I tried to call and tell her what had happened. All she would say was, "You are supposed to be in the church, but I have never seen church people act like you. Does your pastor know you act like that?"

Many people think that just because you go to church and love the Lord, Christians are punks, and we are supposed to allow people to run over us and not say or do anything. WRONG, so wrong. When have you ever read in the Bible that Christians were punks? Peter was no punk, David was no punk, and Jesus surely was not a punk! I do not know where people get that impression from. Never let anyone treat you or talk to you in any kind of way because if you let them do it once, they will continue to do it all the time. Being hurt is not a good feeling.

So, I said I would love my family from a distance.

Chapter Nine

WHAT TOOK THE CAKE

About a couple of months later, my mother returned from Louisiana to visit Virginia. My mother wanted me to come to my third sister's house to spend the night with her… so I did. When I arrived, I parked behind my sister's vehicle. The next morning, my sister got up for work, went outside, then came back inside yelling. It was around 6:00 in the morning.

She yelled, "You parked behind me, you mother fuc%er! Are you crazy? I am the one that got a job. What the hell is wrong with you?!"

I responded, "Oh, my bad."

She then said, "Oh, your bad? You're stupid!"

Here I am, trying to wake up out of my sleep to see what was going on and move my car. By the time I got outside, she was gone. Where I parked was not even the problem. She had a lot of space to move her car, and she did. But that day is what "took the cake" for me. That was the end of my going back to her house, eating out with her, or anything else. I was done for good.

My mom did not believe what I said, of course. She would just say, "Don't pay her no mind."

I told my mom, "Oh, I am going to pay her some mind." I was tired of people talking to me in any kind of way, men using me, and people controlling me. I was done with her, the church, and the men. I refused to continue living like that. I had had enough. Something had to give, and it had to start with me.

I left the church, and I was hurt in all sorts of ways. I had no one to trust, no one to turn to, and I felt God had turned on me too, but I kept praying and believing for a better day. It was so hard. I wanted to return to my old ways so badly, but there was no use. Once again, I had given up for a moment and did not care anymore. But I knew I had come too far to stop. This was a time in my life that I encouraged myself. I had to pick myself back up all over again. I applied for 18 apartment places, and they all turned me down. I did not have a car, but after all, I had been through this time, I said, "This is nothing." I refused to give up. I refused to accept failure. I refused to lose.

I kept going forth. At times, it looked like I just was not going to make it. I kept being faithful to God. It got hard, but I repented and kept moving on. I kept praying and reading the Word. I knew God was telling me that it was no use to give up and that He did not intend for me to lose. In my head, I thought there was no use, and I should just give up and die like I was going to do a long time ago, but I couldn't... no, not this time. I was used to going through what I had to go through. I said to myself; *I will get through this*. I told God, when I was living with my second sister and sleeping on the floor after leaving the church, that I did not belong to these people; I belonged to God.

After I redefined my life and who I was in it, I said I wanted more. I forgave myself and turned my life back over to God.

It had been five years since I had been intimate with a man. I knew no one but God could have done that for me. I never took another drink after I started changing my life.

A New Me, New Way, A New Walk, A New Look, A New Smile, A New Day, A New Talk, A New Mind, A New Heart, A New Life, A New Direction ... The Truth Through Jesus Christ.

As much as I craved my mother's affection and attention, God honestly had another plan for me. Believe it or not, I actually reached that pivotal moment when I realized my life deserved the best. This time around, I was excited and optimistic. I went back to school and finally took my GED test. I was kind of scared because I thought I would be the oldest in the class. But oh no, I wasn't... LOL! There were people there in their 50s. I was amazed, but it was a good thing. I passed and got my GED, and went off to college. When I did, and my family found out, did I get all those things that were promised to me (a laptop, a thousand dollars, etc.)? Ha! No, I did not. I barely got congratulated. That was that. I did not care anymore. I was moving on. In that same year, I received funds... blessed be to God. I was able to pay off the money owed from the eviction and more. I did not even have to pay it all. I owed them $3,500, and I only had to pay $1,200. The lady at the office was so sweet to me.

I went to apply for an apartment again. They called me back three days later and told me I was approved for the apartment. I was so happy. The next day, I got a car. Not only that, but God worked on the inside of me through all that pain, bitterness, and everything else I had. When those painful

56

thoughts resurfaced, and they did, I had to remind myself of who I was and that God had been with me the entire time. It was not my mom, it was not my dad, it was not my sister, and it was not my pastor who had been covering me my entire life. It was God who covered me. It was so amazing, I cried.

I started college, met with a counselor, and chose my degree. I was excited and ready. It was so good for me to be in a class with other college students. Some told me that they did not want to be there. They said they were only there to please their parents. Some said their parents said if they did not go to school, they would take them off of their insurance and lose their car and even their apartment. One student told me her parents wanted her to become a doctor, but she wanted to be a singer. I asked her why she was going to school to be a doctor when singing was what made her happy. She leaned over her chair, rolled her eyes, and said, "I come from a family where they want the best for their kids, nothing but the best, and their kids have to marry the best.

I said to myself, "Wow. I thought I had problems." I had my apartment and what I needed.

I started visiting churches and took my time with it this time around. I pursued my goals, even with writing this book. I was on my way to visit one of the top schools in the United States. I never thought I would be visiting this place, but the Lord said there was nothing too hard for him (Jeremiah 32:17), and I believe that. I began to see what a wonderful woman I was. I began to work out, pray, and eat right. That made a difference in my life. I started looking different, dressing differently, and making a difference in my life. I knew that God never left me. I just had to return to Him, that's all. I was never alone because the Lord said, I will never leave you nor forsake you... I had to get that in my heart and believe it, not just say it because it sounds good. Everyone knows that scripture, but they do not always apply it. You must know that God cannot use anything that has not been broken.

I began to love myself... how did I do that? I began to find out what I liked. I took my self out to eat and to a movie. I began to love myself and put my dreams first. Know that you never have to put your dreams on hold for anyone. Do it now. Oh yeah, it is possible. Going back to school is possible and having a good education is possible. I was learning so much.

Yes, I still think about my dad, but I just try to think of the good times, not many, just a couple. For example, when he told me always to remember that he loves me and his smile. It took me a long time to forgive many people, but I knew I had to so I could move on with my life.

When you have not forgiven someone, they have control over your life. You find yourself thinking about it all of the time. Then, you cannot even sleep at night. If you are thinking about things that happened to you 10, 20, or even 30 years ago, you have to talk to someone about it. Not just anyone, but someone you can trust. For me to forgive and to be free, I had to confess what I had been hurting from. I had to talk about it and cry it out. I was so tired of pretending to be happy. It is no fun. A lot of people have to find ways to make themselves feel good.

I wanted real happiness. Many people sometimes want to talk about us when we make mistakes. We all have made mistakes. There is no little sin or big sin. Sin is sin, whether it is talking about other people or using bad language, etc. I had gotten to the point where I disliked church people. When someone wants to talk about the Lord and say, "I go to this or that church," or "You should come to my church," I would get tired of hearing that. At least 20 people say, "Oh, I have the best church." I was tired of hearing that. I was tired of fake church folk. I was tired of people saying they loved the Lord, but they were always talking about others and smiling in your face while talking about you later. That is what I hated the most.

I wonder what the Lord is really thinking about what is happening in churches today. Churches are forcing people to give, and I do not know why. If you are not giving from your heart, it won't matter anyway, right?

When I had to live in that group home, and from place to place, at times, I thought it was the most terrible thing that could ever happen in my life. See, the things that we think are bad for us in our lives, God really is turning them around for our good.

About two years after leaving the group home, God placed it on my heart to begin sponsoring group homes every year. The first year I did it, I received so much help from other people, like toothpaste, toothbrushes, socks, and so much more. I would cook a lot of food and take many more gifts for them. I would speak to the ladies at home about not letting their past control them and about how I lived in a group home before. I loved it, and the women loved it too. We had a blessed time. I would not be doing what I am now if I had never lived in that group home that I thought was so bad for me. I am doing something positive with what I thought was bad.

Now, you know there always has to be someone with something negative to say, like my third sister. When my sister, mom, and I went out to eat, I asked them if she would like to donate something to the group home. My sister said, "How in the hell are you gonna talk to someone else about life when you got your GED at the age of 23? You don't have anything."

I answered, "I don't have to have anything to give but my testimony." She rolled her eyes, and my mom said nothing, like always.

This is why I say you have to watch who you are around, even the people in your family. I kept going forth in what God called me to do. Does it hurt when people do you like that? Yes, it does. But you just have to continue to move forward. All the negativity that was around was trying to deter me. When that happened, I would just listen to this song called "He Saw the Best in Me." That song fits my life so much. The entire time, even when people put me down and even when I did not believe in myself, God still saw the best and the excellence in me. He showed me that I was somebody. So, what I went through was only to get me to reach back and help someone else who was currently in, or who had been in, my situation. God said his thoughts about us are good and not evil, and I thank Him for it.

Chapter Ten

LOSING A JOB

osing a job... I have lost plenty of them. When I lost these jobs, did I cry? Did I feel bad? Did I just want to go and jump off a cliff? Sometimes I cried, felt bad, and wanted to jump off a cliff because the rent was due. I did not jump off a cliff because I did not put all my trust into a job. On many jobs, they do not give a "snoop" about you. I remember one time at my job, a lady who had been working there for ten years died. She was a young girl. The management barely talked about it. I did not even see a card or flowers sent to her family. I said, "Wow."

The workers there would bust their butts running and working non-stop. Those 18-25 years old looked like they were about 40 years old. I never put my trust in a job. I always had a plan that I did not want to work for someone else my entire life. My trust was not in a job. It paid my bills, some of them. My trust was in God and in believing in myself to do something better with my life, such as starting my own business, writing books, and doing everything else I wanted. But I had to work.

At my job, I was treated like a slave. I hated being treated like that. For example, my old manager would talk to me as if I was crazy and as she owned me. That was another thing that pushed me so much. When she needed me to do something, she would come over to me, snap her fingers, and say, "I need you to go in the Halloween department." She would say it really fast with an attitude and then just walk off. She had an attitude like if she owned you and you needed her. I would feel as if these people were better than me. My manager was taking pills for depression, anxiety, and all kinds of things because she was depressed. I came to realize they were no better than I was. I needed to stop putting myself down. This job just became a means for me to survive.

Use the Gifts God Has Given You

I wanted more than that. I needed more than that. I was living paycheck to paycheck, barely paying rent, my car needed work, and I was just struggling. I did not like that. In fact, I hated it. I was thankful for having a job and a car, but there was more in me… and more in you. Take your gifts and use them. Don't waste them. You are not a waste. Sometimes, we just need someone to encourage us and tell us that God still loves us. GOD LOVES YOU! He has never left you and He will never go away. Leap out into your destiny and do what you were called to do. Was I in fear? OH YEAH! I was so afraid of success. I had lived in poverty for so long. I never saw anyone in my family make it big. At times, it did not feel real. I was afraid of what would happen and what people would think. I was in fear and nervous, and most of the time, I would think of bad things rather than good things.

I have lost jobs, and my family has put me out on the streets. I have lived in shack homes in the winter with no heat and with various people from place to place… and I was able to get through all of it.

Walk Into Your Season

Your season is already here. I had a drive; I believed in myself. JUST KNOW YOU HAVE TO GO THROUGH SOMETHING TO GET TO WHERE YOU NEED TO BE. Just know that God does not mean any harm in your life. He can only use what has been broken. He said that His thoughts about you are good and not evil. So, if you have lost a job, and I know I can say it will be alright, and you are one paycheck from being homeless, or you cannot feed your children, know that I have been there. There were times when I could not feed myself. You have to look for a better day. Believe that God will send you what you need.

Your Test Will Be Your Testimony

We all have to go through something... Jesus did, so why not us? Remember that there is a time and season for everything, so if you or your husband have lost a job, do not give up and do not give in. Just say, "We all have to go through something." At times, God is trying to get you to see Him rather than that job. Maybe you were not spending that much time with your children or spouse, and they needed you. However, your job has your time and your mind. God can't even get to you. So, do not look at the bad side of losing a job; focus on the good side of it. Maybe your job loss is a way of God moving you to start your own business, write that book, or promote that CD. Remember, it is what God wants and not what you want. Pray, because God hears you. Just because He does not answer that day does not mean He will not answer you… He will, in some way. I am that testimony (smile).

Chapter Eleven

BAD CHOICES

How many times in life do you keep making bad choices? I can remember when I was in the lonely stages of my life. I began talking to an older man, knowing he was not for me. He was not even all that attractive by a long shot. Talking to him caused me to lower myself to the lowest. He was a liar of all liars. For example, he would tell me he was coming to pick me up and take me out; I would get dressed up and wait on him, and he would never come. He did this five or six times. You know what? It was not always his fault. It was his fault when he did it the first and second times. I believe in second chances, but it was my fault after that.

A man will only do to you what you allow him to do. The same goes for a man... a woman will only do what you let her do to you. I knew this guy was talking to other women. MAN!! If you could only see the text messages in his phone that I read. Ooops! Did I just say that? Yes, I got his phone and read them. Was I wrong? Maybe and maybe not, but that told me everything I needed to know. I made a choice to continue to talk to him. I did not want to, but on those days when I did not have much to do, I would call him. I knew it was wrong, plus he liked to talk to married women and did these things in front of his 16-year-old son. For me to still be there was wrong and ungodly, and I knew I was. He would talk nasty to all kinds of women. He went to Las Vegas with married women, and I knew these things. So, there was clearly something wrong with me. I had an awesome future, and I should not have wasted my time with him. So, yes, something was going on with me.

I found myself where I could not pray or think straight. I just thought He was not listening to me. But of course, I would think that. All the sin I was in caused me not to know when I would get it together. I degraded God; after all, He did for me and was doing for me. He loved me, and I still did not do what I was supposed to do.

Chapter Twelve

REFUSE TO LOSE

I am the new me. When God manifested in my life, He executed a miraculous turnaround in me. I smiled and laughed. I am amazingly happy.

God gave me a new look and a new heart. I know I have a purpose in life, and now is the time to bring that to light. I made a special commitment to myself not to worry about what others think or say about me. There is so much negativity in this world, and I must remain focused. My main objective in life is to love Jesus Christ and focus on when He returns. When He opens the gates of heaven, I want to be standing right there because I have lived my life righteously. I knew I really loved the Lord. I wanted to live my life right.

It once snowed so much in Virginia. I needed a ride home from work because I did not know how to drive in the snow. I was not used to it. I knew a guy who could take me home, so I called him and asked him to pick me up. I thought that was really nice for him to do because I would have done the same for him. He knew how to drive in the snow because he was from Chicago, where they get a lot of snow. As we were returning to my house, we got lost because he wanted to take the way he wanted. You know, those types of folks who think they know it all? I told him to go my way, but he went his way. He said his way was faster, but we ended up getting lost. We drove for about two hours. He finally got on his GPS and found his way back to where I lived. We drove for about three hours. It was icy and snowing really bad outside.

We finally made it to my house. The snow got worse… it was so bad. I asked him if he wanted to stay for a while and have some cocoa, juice, or something. He said, "Yes, that would be a good idea."

Before he came into my house, he wanted to smoke a cigarette. In my mind, I thought, "I do not want to be around that." If you have been delivered from something and do not want to return to it, then you should not be around it. For example, if you have been delivered from alcohol, you should not hang out at a bar.

He came to my house, and I gave him some juice and a blanket. He ended up falling asleep on the sofa. About two hours later, he awoke and said, "Okay, now are you going to give me some sex?"

I looked at him and responded, "What?"

He repeated it, "Now are you going to give me some?"

I said, "No, I am not."

He said, "So you mean to tell me I drove three hours in the snow to bring you home, and you are going to say no?"

I said, "That's right. I am not going to sell myself short like that."

He said, "When you texted me for a ride home did I tell you no?"

I just looked at him. In my mind, I thought, "Who does this guy think I am?" I asked him, "Am I supposed to give you some because you gave me a ride home?"

He said, "Yup."

I said, "Unbelievable; wow!"

He said, "Nothing in this life is free." Then, in a softer tone, he said, "You are going to need a ride to work in the morning, aren't you? You need your car fixed, don't you? You are going to need to call me again, aren't you?"

I was sitting there listening and thinking, "Yeah, I am." Then he touched my shoulder, and I thought to myself, "Am I going to put my trust in God's words or trust and rely on this guy?" Then I told him, "No, get your hands off me." I just could not do it.

I know I have made some mistakes in my life, but I would not let that night be one of them. He kept asking, trying to persuade me. He said, "C'mon." He said it about 10 times in a forceful way. I wanted him out of my house. He then said I was full of it. He curses a lot and is very disrespectful. He got his jacket and left.

I said, "Be careful going home."

He said, "F_ck that!" He did not even close my door.

I know that I did the right thing, and God sees that. I have been through too much and have seen God come through in my life. I would rather miss working the next day than sell myself short like that.

Ladies, do not ever sell yourself short and feel you have to sleep with a man just because he took you out on a date and bought you dinner. If he is interested in you, he will not force you or make you feel that you have to do anything you do not want to do. Some people may say, "Hey, you gotta do what you gotta do." I believe you have to do what God wants you to do. A real man of God would not want a woman who was that cheap anyway. And for a ride home? Aw, please! We have to value ourselves and watch whom we enter into relationships with. Friends do not matter; we have to watch the company we keep.

Chapter Thirteen

PUTTING THE PAST BEHIND ME

T hroughout my entire life and the things that I have done, God has said to me, "There is nothing new under the sun" (Ecclesiastes 1:9).

I did not do anything too different from or worse than those other women in the Bible. I came from a dysfunctional family; I suffered from depression, bitterness, loneliness, and a chronic inability to forgive myself. I was always uncertain about my life and meditated on my mistakes. I thought of myself as a failure and had suicidal thoughts because I predicted no future, hope, and way out. I was a middle school dropout. I never went to high school and did anything that high schoolers do. I have never been to a prom or had any friends. I never held my head up. I had no reason to.

I was always told that I would never be anything in life and never go anywhere. I was constantly called ugly and a failure. I gave away what was precious to me, but I did not know it at the time… and neither did the men. This was not conducive to my life. It was difficult living without a father's affection. My mother could not love me like I needed to be loved because she consistently endured the abuse rendered by my father. My mother never tried to encourage me to be the best at anything. Even as I grew older, I wished I had gotten what I needed from my parents.

One day, I rented a movie that I love so much. It became my favorite movie. It was called *Gifted Hands*. Wow, I loved it so much. The mother in the movie encouraged her children until the end. She told them they were not losers and would be someone in life, even when the children could not see it or believe it. She may not have had much... even had her own embarrassing issues, but she always kept her faith in God. She always told her children that God would never leave them. As I watched that movie, I sat back and said, "I wish I had a mother like that." Then again, after thinking further about it, I said to myself, "God does not make any mistakes. What I went through and who He used to bring me into this world was no mistake." I had to love and forgive my mother.

I do love my mother, but I put the past behind me. It was a day-by-day process for me because, at times, in my mind, those past thoughts would surface, but I would also think about how God kept and continues to keep me. Look at me now and how God is still taking care of me. I have no reason to stay angry. We all have made mistakes, but at the time, I thought if my mother had been more supportive, my life would have been better... today, I am better.

I have learned to forgive. It is not easy, but prayer changes things. Pray... it works, and it helps. The truth is I felt that nothing ever worked out for me. No one could give me the care that I needed. I remember how I would ask God, "Have you forgotten about me?" I knew I could not change what happened to me in my life, but I could change the future and more. I could not continue to dwell on my past, which kept me bound and chained. I was in bondage. It is amazing to me how no one really knows what someone goes through—the sleepless nights, the heartaches and pain, the low self-esteem, and not to mention the late-night cries for help or just from pain.

I was so embarrassed about what had happened to me in my life. Many times I felt that I was not going to make it. I have been through so much, especially with my family. They knew nothing about the pain, misery, heartbreak, and tears that had fallen from my eyes. I have even cried in front of them, and I still did not have one shoulder to lean on… I was all alone. Sometimes I asked God, "Why? Why? Why?" repeatedly. I thought it would have been much easier if I had help from a loving mother and father like most kids my age had. Although both my mother and father were in the home, they were not the epitome of a family. My mother did the best she knew, considering the make-up of the man she was supposedly raising us with. Even when people would call me and ask me why I would not talk to my third sister, it was not that I did not want to talk to her, but with all the things she had done, I concluded that you could not change people. I believe that she had a telephone just like I did.

Take a look at this… if you are always mean and have negative things to say out of your mouth to someone, and you cannot control your attitude or ever admit that you are wrong about anything that you do, but you want someone to give you hugs, and you tell others that no one likes or loves you, then I wonder they? Maybe you should take a look at yourself— examine yourself. You will not make it far with that kind of attitude and thinking. Do not continue to allow people to hurt you mentally and physically. Know that you deserve better.

Chapter Fourteen

PRAY FOR YOUR ENEMIES

I read about Jesus and how He survived when He was in Samaria. I also read about Daniel in the Lion's Den and Job when he was very ill. Each of these men endured and overcame God. The Bible talks about how you must excel in whatever situation you are placed in, knowing that God will bring you out. For instance, if you are celibate, you should be content. It will be revealed when God gets ready to send you a mate that He has ordained for your life. I would talk to anyone just to fulfill that passion for companionship and the need for love. I should have realized that all I needed was the fullness of God. He will direct my path. I must stop complaining and start confessing. When I do that, I can think more clearly and make better choices in my life. I simply have to endure my personal situation to get to my destiny.

People in my life have really tried to control me rather than encourage me. It was difficult to keep a positive attitude, yet I knew that negativity was not what God intended for my life. Remember, regardless of the situation you are in, you have to do as Jesus did... call those things that are not as though they were. Act like Jesus would act. Pray for your enemies and those who curse, misuse, and reject you. At times I know that can be the hardest thing to do because you feel that something bad should happen to your wrongdoers. Perhaps you want God to send them straight to hell, but remember that we all have made bad life choices.

Chapter Fifteen

YOU GOT TO GO
THROUGH IT

At times, we go through things in our lives, and we complain. I thought about this. We complain about what we go through but look at Jesus and what He did. So, what makes us so special that we will not go through things in our lives? All you have to do is think about Jesus.

I know in my life, I was carrying too much. I had to make up my mind that I would let it go. To not let go was making me feel too bad and weak. I had to find a way, so I prayed with all my heart. I had to find true forgiveness and move on. I was getting a lot of people into my life who did not need to be there. I knew I had to cut those people off. I was not meeting truly saved people. I was meeting folks trying to take me back to who and where I was before. That was not cool. I did not want to go back. It was sickening for me.

Make sure you know the company you keep, and be careful whom you share your dreams with. Those out there are dream killers who will try to hold you back. Some people will try to hinder you from going forth because they feel they cannot go any further in life. Do not compare your life with theirs. Never do that. Remove yourself from people who are not trying to go anywhere in life. It is very important whom you surround yourself with. You will have people who say they want you to go higher, but they really do not. I call those types of people "haters." I knew when the time came to let those people go.

Chapter Sixteen

LOVING HER

I arrived at the point where it was time to let go of the old. I have heard many people say that they wish their parents were still alive and how much they miss them. Now, they do not have the opportunity to tell their parents that they love them and forgive them for what they did or didn't do. My mom is still alive, and I want to take this opportunity to tell her that I love her. I want her to forgive me, also. I want what happened in the past to stay there. Even though I am far from my mother, I call her daily. I can talk to her about things that I thought we would never be able to talk about. Not everything, but most things. We get along… we laugh, and I love her. I want my mother to be a part of my life. When we do not get along, I say, "I love you anyway," and we make up. I did not get to do this with my father. God knows I wish I could have. I did not have the time or the day, but now it is too late. However, I now have the time and day to do this with my mother and sisters.

I know some of you might say, "Well, my mom is on drugs," or "she is a prostitute," or "my mom does not listen to me," or "she acts like she never made a mistake or did anything wrong in her life." You may ask, "How do I love her amidst all of this?"

Well, I understand that all of this is hurting you, and even as time passes and you get older, you must get on your knees and cry out to the Lord. As you feel the pain in your heart and think about what has happened in your life, know that when you find it in your heart to forgive your mother or father, you are doing it for yourself. You will see a change in how you feel about life.

IT'S TIME

There comes a time in your life when it is time to let go, forgive others, and forgive yourself. As long as you refuse to forgive the person who hurt you, they will continue to have control over your life. I forgave my mom. I said, "Lord, I forgive her, and I hope she forgives me too." We cannot go back to all those years. She cannot make up those childhood and teenage years. But I say, "Lord, she only did what she knew, and now, I want a relationship with her, even if it is not with other family members or friends. You cannot make people understand. You have to forgive them and move on… it is up to them to forgive you. You cannot make someone love you, either. I could not keep going through life blaming my mom and dad for what they did not do for me. I had just to do it for us women.

As women, we are so emotional sometimes to the point that we settle for anything. For example, our bodies are a temple, so we should not allow them to be used as a trashcan that can be dumped into at any time. Ha! That is not love. When you love God, you can love yourself, and only then can you really love someone else. He can show you who you are. When you begin to love who you are no matter what, you will not need anyone's approval. At times, we ladies try to make a relationship work. You cannot make that man love you anymore. A real man of God will not make you do anything outside of the will of God. Pray about everything first.

I used to be afraid to ask God about some men because I never knew he would want me to be in a relationship. I just did not pray about that. I did not want God to tell me that it was not my season or my time for dating while I was a full-time student, working, writing, and loving Him. Well, ladies, I say to you, love yourself. Never put your dreams on hold for anyone or for any relationship. Go after what you want, don't settle. So many times in life, we go from one relationship to another. We are so used to being in one and being with someone that it feels weird when we are not in a relationship. I have learned in my life that you cannot make people believe in you. I learned to forgive through the pain. I learned to forgive so I could move on. You have to know what you are moving from. You have to know where you come from and where you are going and that where you come from has NOTHING to do with where you are going.

Conclusion

REFUSE TO LOSE

Congratulations on beginning your new spiritual journey. I pray that this word has blessed, inspired, empowered, and motivated you. I hope you have enjoyed reading it more than I have enjoyed writing it. I hope your journey does not end here but rather that this story will encourage you to move forward in your life.

Remember, encourage yourself, Love yourself. Some may ask, "How do I encourage myself, even when no one else does?" SELF-LOVE. Just because others seem like they are winning before you first, do not mean you are losing. You lose when you give up.

WHAT WILL YOU REFUSE?

List 10 things below that you will refuse ...

Example: I refuse to be in a relationship that is one-sided.

1.
2.
3.
4.
5.
6.
7.
8.
9.
10.

PUBLIC APPEARANCES

Demetria Buie is available for:
~ Speaking Engagements ~
~ Book Signings ~

To request Ms. Buie for your pajama party, Lupus awareness community, organization's function, Conference, Retreat, Parties, birthday pop-ups, book signings with meet and greet virtual Events and classes or for private Writing consultation, please contact her @t Aintnolosing36@yahoo.com.

Thank you for your interest.

I do not have all the answers, nor have I arrived or ever will. I will forever be evolving, learning, and growing.

And I'm sharing what I've learned in hopes I will support you in keeping your own connections, finding your own journey, but mostly the Love within yourself. In my next book, I will go deeper within you to help you find yourself and share my new journey...

Meditation Guidance

Self-Love Affirmations

Wealth Affirmations

Marriage Affirmations

Love Affirmations

New friends Affirmations

Here I am again. So much has changed. I'm not her anymore. I'm on a new journey. So much I had to let go and leave behind. Who am I now? Whom have I become? The new journey was scary, but it was necessary. It was an unfamiliar place. My spirit that deep inner me knew I couldn't stay in the old... I grew. I loved. I flew. I asked myself what did this new look like. I felt. Change, isolation, sacrifice, & Removal. Success came from Removing people, things, and places.. I actually learned the hard way. At 37, I finally got some of it, but not all. Peace. Love. Joy.

I cared too much... about people; what they thought of me; I let people down; tell me what I could and couldn't have. How far I could go. Even told me I didn't have a choice in life and that I had to settle because I had gained weight! Told me what I needed didn't matter. What I desired, I wouldn't get. The removal was necessary. I knew the inner me; I knew what I wanted and what I could have. The sky was the limit for me... but there were some I needed to take and listen to. Grab your copy of my new book. From Broken Woman To Business Woman of the steps I took & the changes I had to make in my life. God, the Lord Jesus Christ, knew what I needed. All I had to do was follow!!

Raw Chapters of my life...

The Authentic Me I became! I needed her.

Affirmations.

Meditation.

Change of foods.

My workouts.

My water.

My skin.

1. Stop explaining yourself to people.

2. Stop getting validation from others.

3. Stop telling your business to people.

4. Stop connecting to people because you need a friend or are lonely. Stop with people who only had regrets in their life & you feel it when you talk to them. Energy. Discernment. Don't feel right.

5. Stop posting and telling you every next move.

6. Stop calling people that couldn't solve your problem. They are in need just as much as you.

7. Stop entertaining what you don't want. Stop going on dates just because someone asks you; you're bored. So many people have settled, and I definitely was that person! This advice might not be for everyone, but it's for someone.

8. Mind my own business. Everything people do ain't my business.

9. Stop taking on assignments that I wasn't called to take upon.

10. Get away from people that don't bring you joy & peace!!...

11. All money ain't good money. Stop signing contracts with difficult-drama people. I don't care how much they are paying you; you do not deserve to be disrespected and go through hard stress.

12. Doing more doesn't always equal success. When I started doing less, I have seen more money and peace!!...

13. Be okay that this journey can be lonely. Be okay without responding negatively about you or your new life!

14. Know the real example of a leader.

15. Don't just quote stuff because you heard the crowd or it sounds good. Quote, stuff that you actually believe, understand, and Live it!

16. Enjoy the process if you don't like hearing this. You ain't ready!! Rather it's working out. Just enjoy working out and buying new cute workout outfits. The results are powerful.

17. Protect your peace and energy!!...

18. BELIEVE!!! TAKE ACTION on what you say you're gonna do without excuses.

People always say I can't do this or that because I don't have time or money. You ain't ready!!

When I was 9 years old, my dad gave me a beer... YEAP!! I think it was old English. Now, my mom didn't know about it lmao. My. My. Lol, and told me never to let my left hand know what my right hand was doing. And to never let anyone know what I was doing next or your next move... I mean, I'm 9. I didn't understand that! My goodness. I understand now!!...

19. Get off everyone's prayer line and platform. Remember, these were for ME!!

20. Release without revenge!!... Forgive without bitterness!

21. Know what you want in life & be very clear...

Remember, in this life, Entrepreneurs, industry, People will love you today and cancel you tomorrow.

Lastly: Know who you are. Know the power that you hold. Know your purpose while here on earth & fulfill it!!!

Stop worrying about everyone else business and which to sleep with whom... talking about people all the time. Always on the phone got something to say...

I met this girl one time, and she always knew everyone posted on Social Media from 2 platforms, she always knew everyone.

Business and how, when, and who. She was always talking about people, folk's business, and EVERYTHING. I'm like, lorrrddd!! I was completely tired of that relationship. Had to end it!! I tried to hold on, but... she was too much. I was trying to figure out how she has the time or that kind of energy. My. My...

A lot of things couldn't work or happen for me because everything I did was to please other people. I was literally afraid to me. But when I got out of my way and realized that the only person who was keeping me from my destiny was ME!!

Exactly what you dreamed. Better than you imagined.

God can do excitedly abundantly above what you ask or imagine...

1. Decide what you really desire.

2. Visualizing having what you desire.

3 . Start being thankful for having what you desire.

It was told that the broker you are, the more blessed you are. The more I chose partners that weren't wealthy and didn't have their necessary stuff together, that was exactly what I needed, and God would bless it... and as long as I was loved, that's all that mattered. Do you know it takes more than Love to keep a marriage together? See... the things we were taught. Chillleee, you can't be out here just dating anybody just because they asked, and it's a free meal hunni noooo... stop dating what you don't want. YOU ARE HOLDING YOURSELF BACK!! After my last Divorce, I knew the time for me and my vagina to take a BREAK!! No dating. No nothing... I learned so much within me during these 3 years...! Self-love attracts LOVE!!...

GO GRAB THE BOOK!!!

At 37, as I look in the mirror, and I'm like, wow, I'm just finding out what true love is. God is Love; he loves me, and self-love is love. Now I know what loving someone else truly is. Becoming a mother has taught me many things about Love, sacrifice, and selflessness. I have not yet arrived, nor will I ever. I will forever be a student ready and willing to learn no matter how much I learn and get n life. I ask God to give me forever the strength to keep going!!!....

"Only if I was privileged."

God, why wasn't I privileged? Throughout my life, I looked at other girls and saw how their mom/dad gave them everything they wanted. Mom/Dad had money, a big home, and even a luxury car, and I saw girls wear whatever they wanted to wear.

God, why did I have to be homeless? Why did I have to see my dad in jail? Why didn't I love myself? God, why didn't I have parents who flew me around the world and showed me what I could be in life?

The End.............

5 minute journaling

5 minute journaling

5 minute journaling

5 minute journaling

5 minute journaling

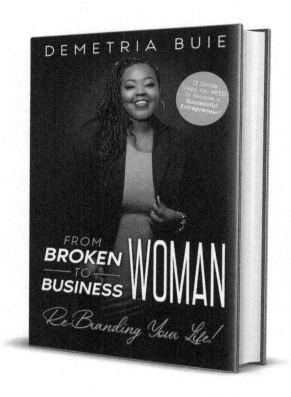

Chillleee Sit Down & Pour Yourself A Glass,
You Might Need Two.

Made in the USA
Columbia, SC
29 October 2024

45027837R00063